P9-EDE-700

SONG IN
A STRANGE
LAND

SONG IN A STRANGE LAND

George Keithley

GEORGE BRAZILLER

NEW YORK

LIBRARY
The University of Texas
At San Antonio

ACKNOWLEDGMENTS

Grateful acknowledgment for permission to reprint these poems is made to the editors of the following publications: *The Branch* for "Buying the Black Hills," "A Song for Survivors," and "On Clark Street in Chicago"; *Cat Fancy* for "Look You're Laughing"; *Choice* for "The Big Rock Candy Mountain," "Black Hawk in Hiding," "The Hill Coast," and "Lines on Eliot's Death"; *Cutbank* for "Riding Home"; *The Galley Sail Review* for "The Cheyenne Station"; *Harper's Magazine* for "Buster Keaton & the Cops" and "How Crazy Horse Was Killed"; *The Iowa Review* for "Lincoln in Love," "Passing the Night," and "A Song for New Orleans"; *The Literary Review* for "Morning Star Man" and "The Nomination of Abraham Lincoln"; *The Magdalene Syndrome Gazette* for "November as the New Moon"; *The Massachusetts Review* for "After Antietam," "Charlie Chaplin Has the Last Laugh," "The Fillmore," "The Land of the Dead," "With King in Memphis," and "You Are Never Happy"; *Noise* for "A Song for Salt Lake"; *The North American Review* for "After His Assassination a Place of Peace"; *Prairie Schooner* for "Depot Song"; *The Sweet Thief* for "Born in Chicago," "Mardi Gras," "The Superior Court," and "The Wind"; *The Yale Review* for "A Photo by Brady"; and *Yankee* for "The Great Northern Railway."

A portion of the preface appeared in *Rolling Stone*.

For
Liz and Clare and Chris

"How can we sing the Lord's song
in a strange land?"
—*Psalm 137*

CONTENTS

I
The Right to Rise Up

II
I Shall Vanish and Be No More

III
Who Will Want Railroads?

IV
Early Life

V
Democratic Times

VI
What Is the Wild Love that Leads Us?

CONTENTS

PREFACE

These forty-nine poems present scenes of American life from the young manhood of Lincoln to our own time—a sequence of poems in the continuity of a song. It is the second in a series of four volumes, begun by *The Donner Party,* an epic told in a linear narrative. *Song in a Strange Land* is concerned with the atmosphere of our life from that era to the present. The third volume will concentrate on the life cycle in a single community, and a fourth book related to these will follow.

If the climate of the country is too turbulent for a single form to suggest, some structure across time and shifting scenes is needed to express it. I sought a sequence which depicts the past merging with the present . . . For example, at the outset we were at war with ourselves while we possessed the land, to use Frost's phrase. With the arrival of industries such as the railroad, we left the land for the steel and mobility of modern life. Still in much of our life the abandoned land asserts its claim on us.

I believe this experience and others can be suggested in song—lyrics, monologues, narratives, ballads—poems of many people, a few eloquent leaders, a beautiful and abused landscape. But each poem must produce its own sound, while it contributes to the whole. I admire in poetry its ability to move us by its music—however understated or overwhelming the music may be. Whatever technique is used, the point is to bring the poem to life and let the listener learn of it and feel it at the same time, as we do in the presence of a new song.

The continuity of a song grows from no national virtue or vice, but the individual's voice, speaking or singing in the untracked energy of his own nature. Even before the Civil War we unleashed that force of mobility and unrest which has made our lives more turbulent, and leaves a sense of longing in the land.

I think our struggle over the land is not a history of events but an evolving emotional life. In the solitude of fields and cities we search each other's faces, we hear the speech of regions drawn close by commerce, voices of abundant variety. Yet every visitor in our country is asked, "What do you think of Americans?"—as though the answer will help us to discover what we think of ourselves. A violent history and a restless affection spring from the same soil and thrive in the weather within us. They leave us silent for a time, but from this solitude comes song.

G.K.

I

The Right to Rise Up

Any people anywhere, being inclined
and having the power, have the
right to rise up, and shake off the
existing government, and form a
new one that suits them better. This
is a most valuable—a most sacred
—right, a right, which we hope and
believe, is to liberate the world.

Abraham Lincoln,
U.S. House of Representatives
January 12, 1848

Lincoln in Love

When we hear the song
of two tanagers
and stand in the warm
shade of an elm
it's the same as
it was in my dream.
But in the dream
it was night; yet
the yellowthroats
and two tanagers
were out. We sat
watching them courting
across the river,
chasing each other
beyond the bank. We
said nothing and there
was no need to—
one bird calling and
one bird answering.
But by daylight
whatever they sing
is a mystery.
It means nothing
at all or whatever
it was was lost

in my long ears.
I believe the birds
must know the words
but they won't say.
They like to see
you and me suffer
this way. They enjoy
the chagrin of children
like us. Of course
it won't be better
before it's worse.
They must cherish
the anguish of adults
as much: a man
explaining his marriage
to the darkness
where his dog sits
silent and the mule
waits to eat. In all
the field of natural law
we wade with our feet
submerged in sucking
mud and it seems
we must stop and
sink at any hour
because we are weak
and the only peace
is in our sleep
and the only power
is in our dreams.

4

The Nomination of
Abraham Lincoln

I
The Party Chiefs

The party chiefs wear high hats to the Wigwam Hall
but shed their coats when they begin
to barter for delegates.
The regular faction feel
Lincoln is a born democrat of the same ilk
as the ground-grubbing whigs. Well-to-do
men of several central states
raise one ankle across the other knee,
pulling at a silken stocking, anxiously.

His supporters rise to argue history
will find him among the reliable friends
of the railroads. A moderate, to be sure,
nevertheless a man who stands
for free soil now, and no more slaves in the future.

2
Keeping Order by the River

Outside the hall
a handful of boys burn
banners torn off the wall
of a warehouse. Their bonfire rises from the riverbank.

Near enough to smell the smoke,
a horse patrol crosses over
the Chicago river.

Promptly it returns by the same route,
the police parading
their huge horses back and forth, dividing
the crowd that has clattered out—

People part to let the horses by,
then blend together again in the street cheering,
and hearing the songs they cry carried far away.

3
Street Song

Down the street,
    around
in a ring,
    the children
link their arms
    and sing,

"Hail Columbia,
    happy land!
If you aint
    drunk,
then I'll
    be damned!"

4
*The Departure of
the Delegates*

They start home, baggage swinging in hand.
They smoke away the distrust of the day
and walk under the cool high vault of the station house.
Some are singing as they climb the rubber steps
to a scrubbed steam car, and ride out beyond the coal
   ash—

Delegates drawn beyond the blinding white
grain elevators at the rail yard—
Beyond the farms in mild May already green
and still tender with the late seed corn and grain.

*

The train trembles on the rails as it begins to brake.
A man stretches into his coat.

When he disembarks
the dusk absorbs his pallor on the platform.

Batting at a swarm of lake mosquitoes,
he walks into the warm street, greeting his wife,
who has worn her white dress for this, pressed and
   proud.

*

Past the armory shed
and an army recruitment tent
young men take their torches
around town,

leading a loud throng thru the night—
filling the street in front of the silent stores
and trampling the uneven lawns—
their hasty lamps lighting the fiery crowd.

5
Acceptance Speech

I could not attend our convention unless a victory
was certain. Better to lie low.
Solomon Sturges, the banker, offered me
his hospitality if I should come
to Chicago. I wrote in reply,
"I am a little too much
a candidate to stay home
and not quite enough a candidate to go."
During the deliberations I stood by
in Springfield, marking time:
we knew the nomination was within reach
but I planned no public approach.

I wrote to my managers, "Make no contracts that will
    bind me,"
but they traded for every vote
available. Well-wishers flocked to find me
at our house afterward and deliver

8

their hurrahs. I stepped onto the porch.
In the street a brass band played
"Hail Columbia!" over
and over. *Today's honor did not denote
merit in me but in our cause*—this brief speech
they ignored, however,
shouting above the band until a parade
swept all assembled down the road.

It's appropriate for that multitude to set out alone
to celebrate. After this day
they are not neighbors so much as flesh and bone
broken upon each other, like dry boughs
the gale grinds together. My wife wept
with delight though my own arms
were weighed down by our good news.
To the homeless or lame or dead should I say
we who earn eminence by your blood accept
this honor? When they rise
tomorrow they will accuse us of these crimes,
and we will confess to our names.

A Photo by Brady

His large faith looks like ours and he believes
like us that his camera's report
records nature. The silent lives
of men are filmed where they were flung out
in the sunny grass and the scene achieves
simplicity . . . A flat calm distorts
the field of vision as though the men's
mouths made no more noise below his lens.

On the grey grass or the sky nothing flies
from fear. There's some withdrawal
of smoke, a haze beneath the trees
where the surprised troops fall along the hill.
Each figure rests in an insane ease—
all conscious grace, all that is natural
halted as sunlight floods the aperture.
Heavy flank fire floats in the air.

Wedged against the trees a white
church bleaches the hilltop. With pure
release men sprawl in the grass, prostrate,
their shirts blown open on the pasture.
The long sense of balance is accurate
and quiet . . . A thoughtless leisure
on their legs and groin and arms as the church-ground
takes the sun and their pale breasts burn unbound.

After Antietam

The breeze rises
loud off the crisp grass.
The lame in the field scream prayers, and wait
for the bearers. The kindly, the careful. Arriving now.
The deserters crawl in the long grass.

Upstream, McClellan's pursuit hesitates.
His delay, his bloodless pause, spares
Hood's hard-marched, bone lean forces; and Lee's.
Like rumor, the ghosts of these troop off south.
Rewarded with whisky
Colonel Ferrero's thirsty
51sts drink happily.
Lie on.
            By the Dunker church in the smoking grove
with Lady Jane the regiment's
laughing-stock.
                        Autumn in the mauve wood
the farm girls will rein in
and sit their mounts silent . . .
The ponies lap and blow at the shallow stream.
Sunny hills swell.
                        A detail slips thru the ripe corn
fetching out the shattered horses.
In pens the swine are full for the harvest
butchering and the temperate feasts.
These wait, and again all wait.

My love, lie in the day with me, to the shade
and hour of the sane order, when flesh and flesh
breed history, word of the act: Rodman slain,
his men safe, dry. Burnside baffled.
Cautious McClellan, wary and loving
the men walking in at dusk from the blue copse.
Their dragging, piling motion orderly
clearing cornfield and hayfield of the carcasses
of cavalry-, wheel-, and pack-horses,
arranging memory on the green valley.
Late September down the valley
the wind smoulders the sweet greasy smoke
of the torched horses,
the wind black, the gristle popping.

Arm turned in arm, my love, lie on with me
as the gusty November snow settles
uneasy against the scattered nettles,
across the black hay, the scorched timothy.
Silent as dormant limbs, as the seasons
freeze terrain north to Pennsylvania's hills;
at thaw the seed distending in the soil
sprouts rapid pasture, green to a weak sun!
Out of May the copper stream rills under
the fume of lilac blooming, the arched stone
bridge. The stand of poplar saplings rises
to the oriole. Into the summer
leaning warm, lie on with me, my love, low
springs the wind, tall grow the raving grasses.

A Song for Survivors

A warbler sinks with the light
rain in a startled cloud
of white dogwood blossom.
Silver-locked and slickered
Lee's man murmurs a rare
piece of advice and turns his back
on the troops still at attention:
Slip down home for your women
hold the raptured girls close forever
like honey in your mouth
God spare our dear hearts

If she was a beautiful bitch
of a lady however what good
is the thought of that to you
when the heart is in no hurry
stroll to the lawnswing and talk
what can she say what can you say
it is a hell of a steep walk
out of Richmond to Kentucky
to steal a horse and anyway
a stiff ride to Mississippi
riding down to see what may be
there of Hattiesburg yes
the dogwood profuse on the black lawns

behind the black gates
it is a matter of economy
it is a question of necessity
it is a question of how
gradual and parched the hill
earth is.

What you have (besides
this splint horse now) in Hattiesburg
is history. And she is there
you can fetch her north to Memphis
a decent town a decent job
or see her leave her and ride to
Memphis. Stay in Mississippi
you lie back on a flat field
under the humming sky and see
the wings beating in the branches
and hear the screams arise

(a voice torn out of the trees)

when the butcher birds invade
the shelter of the summer lawn
and promise to perturb for days
the solitude of the ripe heat,
the butcher birds who dive and cry
and disenchant the dying shade.

II

I Shall Vanish
and Be No More

I shall vanish and be no more,
but the land over which I now roam
shall remain
and change not.

Omaha Indian warrior song

He Is Burning

He is burning
to see her, his eyes
are smeared with smoke.
The flame in his flesh

a torchlight which leads
the man home. Four days
on horse from the hunting camp,
the thin huts hung with skins—

unlike those long houses
built of elm bark
in the village where she sleeps
among so many women.

At night now he sees
the meadow of her brown eyes,
her breasts blossom
above the bent grass—

He is burning to hold her
close the way the wind
holds fire in a bush
until it eats down to the dirt.

But by dawn
he hears the whole town
waking—a dozen
or more dogs barking—

Barking at the dawn!
Rides in to find the fields
wild with horses, his hogs
driven from their pen.

The lodges are lit like kindling
for cooking. Fire consumes
all the frames. Walls fly up
as if to outleap their flames.

Men as white as ice
are chasing the children out
of the village to mingle
among the hogs,

the women wading after
in a surf of skirts
and grass, struck
across the back with sticks—

He is burning
to bury his knife
in the breast of the blond lieutenant
leading the raiding party,

who withdraw to their fort
not far from the mouth
of the shrieking river—

Behind them a hundred homes
of the bark of black elms
blazed to the ground
as a precaution
against contamination.

Stragglers return from the fields
and while they gather
the wind weaves the hair
of young and old together

and weaves the braids of water
flowing by their feet—
the river where they see
their faces floating away.

Black Hawk in Hiding

Everyone can see me standing in the center
of the stockade, which I hear was built to contain
white soldiers who got drunk or disobeyed
their officers—now it houses their prisoners of war.
The soldiers grow sober looking at us
in the sunlight over the fence.

*

A chain runs around my wrists and under my balls.
It circles both my legs like an iron vine.
A black bar is fastened to both feet
to make certain I won't run far
and I don't try, I just stand still.

*

I hope I will die soon
so I can go into the woods around Rock river
and stop knee-deep among the mesh
of creepers growing under the trees,
and breathe the brown bittersweet stink
of stale fish and grass, keeping back
in the wet shade where no one can see me.

Morning Star Man

juggles old bones
and odd stones. He lofts these long bones
end over end, and they land in one hand.

The stones he flips fast and high,
higher still, so they will drop
one by one on his other palm.

      Along his spine a red fox fur
      has spread like fire. His thin arms and legs
      sprout small paws on which he prances

      among the maples with a merry smile
      below his snout. When he walks upright
      again it's the grin of a grown man.

In green daylight a kettle is set
upon a rock—level full
of maple syrup steaming hot—

He leans over its brim to thrust
his hand, his wrist, his whole human arm
into the thick liquid while we scream.

The shaman scrubs his skin and shows
how his flesh glows from the heat:
no burns or blisters, no sign of harm.

He calls a young couple to come forth.
The girl refuses to let their eyes meet.
She won't lift her gaze from her feet.

In her hands he lays two figures
carved from wood. Male and female tied
together with one leather thong.

She pries these two apart. Their faces
are their own—hers and the man
looking on, whose heart she will not have.

The belly of the female is a box
hollowed below her bosom to hold
inside her a crouching animal—

the meticulous image of a fox.
She shudders. Then a cold shriek
as she feels the creature within her

and flings herself into the arms
of her neglected lover. Death
alone can loosen their embrace.

Their eyes find only one another.
Their host has burst into flames of hair
that hide his flanks; his ribs bristle.

Into the trembling shade he trots
quickly to cover on all fours,
while his tail flails between his thighs.

*

Asked how he came to make his home
among us, he gives this reply:

"At night did you never see a small
ball of flame hurled out of heaven?

How it scorched poor earth!
The pain my mother bore at my birth—

This fire that flies from the night sky
is no star. Look up— It is I! It is I!"

Buying the Black Hills

Rattlesnakes wriggle out of the limestone
to slide into the sunlight and lie still.

The land below bakes in an eternal sun,
and the brown grass grows up from its soul.

How Crazy Horse
Was Killed

Because there was gold in the Black Hills
people wished to go up and dig, which required a road
running thru the quiet country.
                                    We knew our duty
was to protect the public
and we kept our eyes open for anyone who incited
trouble among the agency indians or the hostiles
who wouldn't come in and live on our land
when they were invited.
                              We had to watch him
in particular because we were told
he had such power with his people.
This wasn't easy to understand.
He stood not much bigger than a boy
and his hair was soft and straw-brown;
his skin was no darker than a white's with a tan.
He ruled himself with terrible restraint
and disliked dancing or wearing paint.
So we thought half-breed but he was a full-blood.
Our informants agreed that he gained
his fame and influence from his visions,
such as the one about his horse

dancing in a wild way on the landscape
of the other world. Hence his name.
Some took these tales at face value,
some had other impressions ... Moreover
he kept so silent it was hard to hear
what he was planning. When we sent spies
they brought back lies to guarantee their salaries.
Well, we needed someone we could trust.

Regardless of the rumors, he was only human;
why not get him a good-looking woman?
So we brought him a half-breed girl and let her live
in the hills at his place. She slipped away
each week to report. I think you'll agree
it was necessary to do this
or we would never have any peace.

2

When she told us that he planned
to leave the territory
we were truly alarmed.
Whether he went away
to hunt awhile or settle
he had to pass among people
whose lives we were sworn to protect,
and no one doubted that he was armed.
Or were we to think he wanted to kill
the elk and bison with his bare hands?
Well, we sent a select party to request
that he visit the fort and discuss

his journey with us. On the way
more of our men rode up to escort him.
It wasn't wise to let him leave
our jurisdiction for any reason. One can say
for certain he knew of the warriors in prison—
he would be watching for his chance to return
and we would never have any peace.

3

Our cannon were concealed
by a wall of cottonwoods, and where the road came up
a river of dust drifted into the trees
as the party proceeded. He rode right by
to the front of the fort. There was no trouble.
He dismounted and followed. We said we were
going to greet the officer in his house . . .
Our plan was just to jail him overnight
and hurry him out of the country under guard.
We wanted a high walkway to the door
so he couldn't see—in this we had the help
of several hundred horse troops
and the local Lakota indian police.
They formed a corridor to the jail
but he heard men dragging their chains,
then he saw the small building with the bars
on the windows and he went out of his head.
He dropped his blanket and showed a knife.
Someone bent his arms behind him
but he slipped free and started to attack
anyone near him, slashing at us

with his blade until he drew blood.
So the sentry stuck a bayonet in his back
and our worries were over. He fell
gently on his face. We slid him inside
and put him to bed, where he died. At sunrise
two people tucked his body in a box
and dragged it into the Badlands to bury him
where no one was watching. Maybe a prairie hen
and her young hunched in a bush—overhead
the eagle hawks kept looping like patrols.

It was just as well. Outsiders will sympathize
with him of course but we had to kill
the fool or fight a new war with his friends.
Or we could give up our guns
and unlock the gates and let everyone run loose
and we would never have any peace.

A Bird Is Whistling
in the Trees

A bird is whistling in the trees
across the creek.
On the bank a young Maidu man
and woman, awake
since dawn, fuss with their fire,
snapping spry twigs
to feed the flame—a rope
of smoke floats
thru the thin mountain air.
After coffee
she offers to cook nothing
else, and they give
it up. Pack up two bedrolls
and soak their coals
with water cupped from the creek.

She watches the sun
light tall pines like torches
beginning to blaze.
Among the trees one brown bat
sails home in the haze
of daybreak. "Find us a house
in town," she says:

"I won't have my baby in these
woods. He won't be
born in the dirt like me."

How can he argue
against her shame? Yet her
anger never
alters her voice. She speaks
still in that same
urgent tone: "Someplace dry
and warm. With one
big bed and our own stove."

In silence they start
like strangers down a steep grade
of poor growth, past
a stand of scrag timber,
the best trees cut
for lumber. Much of the rest
blown over to rot
under rain or snow. No place
his family ought
to live the whole year. Although
he'll admit it
to himself, he won't say so—

Nowhere to go
but hike on into town,
looking for work—
A lumber plant open outside

Oroville, tarpaulin
tied over a few woodpiles.
Two trucks hauling
heavy timber thru the gate.

In a gully below
the road the raw air
of autumn greets
the grass. When they rest here
her dress stretches
taut on her swelling belly,
too high to cover
the tan curve of her thigh.
His hand caresses
her breast which has become
a mound of muscle,
all her nerves are alert.
She rises to comb
her hair like a long veil,
letting it fall
about her blouse. They turn
once more toward town.

Before they reach the streets
she hears him
humming: *Better days
are coming for
you and for me.* Then she
takes up the tune,
but both are out of breath,

they have to laugh
while a breeze blows over
the troubled gully,
over the gulf of their life.

III

Who Will Want Railroads?

And if railroads are not built, how shall we get to heaven in season? But if we stay at home and mind our business, who will want railroads?

Henry Thoreau, *Walden*

The Boxcar

They stand quietly at the door
of a railroad boxcar
found in a field and
holding only hay now. They both listen before
helping each other
enter. A cemetery
stillness settles upon the prairie.
After the young couple
climb into the car, they stoop to gather
enough straw in their arms to make
the modest mattress which he shares with her.

His shirt and her dress are their sheet
spread over their stiff bed
of straw. The sun swells,
hanging overhead. Indifferent to the dark heat
about them, they lie
an hour later on the floor
of the boiling boxcar and ignore
the light leaving the pale
prairie. Body and spirit utterly
lost to the summer life of soil
or sky, and at rest in the dying day.

A red moon rises from these weeds.
At one edge of the field
a dog emerges
in the dusty shower of stubble or dry seeds
he shakes from his hair.
Walking home, they hear his bark
behind them. The moon bays in the dark
as they return to town,
where love lies buried deep in the unclear
souls of men and women waiting
only to lie down, to be born once more.

The Great Northern Railway

The iron exposed like bone begins to cloud,
going blue in the October cold.

The strands of steel starting from St. Paul
float onto the flatlands,
feeling thru the morning frost.

The wind threshes the grass into grains
of golden chaff.

When a black-neck elk wanders out
wearing patches of chaff like snow
melting in the yoke of his mane

no one says a word around the railbed
so he lifts one leg over.

His hoof hits one wood tie,
trying his weight on it
before he will cross the tracks

as though he has heard something—

the miles of silence saying nothing
is coming

and he decides to wade out
into the cold waves of weeds.

When we turn to go
we take the weather with us

leaving

the veins of coldness
the long iron lines of isolation

plunging into the prairie
and sinking under the grass at last.

The Cheyenne Station

I

When will it be winter? We are waiting
for the first snow to glaze the ground,
hiding the high brown grass, piling
pools of pure white water on the rails,
and raising the rotting roof
of the Cheyenne station into heaven where it will grow
invisible, dissolving in the driving snow.

Finally today the flakes
are finding their way thru all the dark
thickets of empty alders—the aspen shake
like outrageous brides' heads, wagging their webs
of white. Look how alone in the park
an old man pisses in the bushes.

2

Two boys tossing a football flinch as it stings
their palms *pock pock* over the tracks.
In the cold they try to flex
their fingers as they walk past
the station and leave
the platform and the loading dock
and wander down
the mountain basin
where the blue shocks
of bunch grass stand up stiff with frost.

3

Two girls run between the rails that lead out
into the dark
and narrow together
until the lines are lost under the range
of mountain shadow, below a scarf of new snow.

They stop running, they grip each other and step
over the soft snow slowly
leaving a double track,
walking not looking up,
their eyes wet with cold
and knowing the moon has crawled into the mountains.
For a moment they are so happy they cannot speak.

Depot Song

One day you have to leave the dead
still in the street, talking outside the stores. Nobody does
the luring, but the heart, and a man's eyes follow

the yellow cars on the railbed
jogging to the south. And one evening a man has
pulled himself into a car and leans his head at the
   window.

I don't like living on all alone,
and the next time you see me I'll be gone.

IV
Early Life

People I meet . . . the effect upon
me of my early life . . . of the
ward and city I live in . . . of the
nation. . . .

Walt Whitman,
Song of Myself

Born in Chicago

We were born in Chicago in the same year,
while the shameful depression outlived
either birth—
yours in the springtime and mine in summer—
but it brought
to our own lives a likeness which survived.

There's a tempo to the walk and speech
of people if it's only
the rhythm of men
and women who pass from street to street
asking each other,
Where do you work? Who says that I'm lonely?

We were children when we learned this song
of longing people carry
out of the country
of conscious life when they're young
and years later
we met and fled into the city to marry.

Hearing the News

Hearing the news
of the war as we sat around the stove,
we were certain my uncle was still alive.
My grandfather felt that he might appear
at any time. My brother said so too.
My father stood up from his chair
and strode out to unlock the door.

Our dog trotted across the floor
and shook the snow off his back.
I brought the spoons to the table.
My mother sipped a little of the soup
and lifted the pan off the flame
as the newscast continued and the dead rose
in number while we listened, keeping warm.

Passing the Night

One winter night in the second world war
I stand beside my brother and stare
at the strangers. These people are
the families of sailors passing
the night in the Northwestern Station,
holding hands and chattering like children
home from school, and hardly aware
of the seamen's bags sunk to the floor
in the lobby.
                    Their voices stop
whenever someone hears the hiss
of an engine or the initial slip
of the enormous wheels.
                              Winter forces
parents to plunge their hands
deep in their pockets as they leave
the passenger gates and grow
interested in the terminal—
the coffee counter or commuter bar
and the all-night newsstands.
Hundreds wander under the wall clock
or browse beside the empty benches,
wasting time and not wanting
to watch the brown cars slide away,
leaving the long shed and slowly
crawling over the country in the snow.

I Knew There Was Nothing Wrong

I knew there was nothing wrong
with eating the sugar beets that fell
off the freight cars. We were crazy
about them, because they were sweet

and they were free— I mean that once
they struck the railroad embankment
and tumbled into the high weeds
they didn't belong to anybody else.
We could keep as many as we could find.

We learned to hold our heads up
and grind the meat between our teeth,
letting the juice drain down our throats
until we couldn't taste any more—
then we sat up and spit out the pulp.

Next day another train rolled by.
For years there was this lavish supply
of sugar beets following the harvest,
but people lost interest after the war.

Riding Home

Riding home in an open jeep
after practice we lean
into a turn, pull back, hold
ourselves straight on the steel seat.

All this country is cold.
You hear hissing heat
only in front, blowing from the brown
box below your knees.

Before the road reaches town
the boy driving sees
a field without fence on one side,
whips the wheel to his right,

and we glide
over gravel shoulder onto the light
surface snow—
the field frozen at the end of fall.

The jeep jumps from furrow to furrow.
Talk of football
or the stories of school girls stop,
riders are flung

onto the stiff farmland where we drop
to our knees. Unharmed among
the frozen rows we find
our footing and shout—

stumbling at nightfall behind
the stalled car. When we walk out
the blood still
in the veins of every voice

of its own will
rises, and we rejoice—
shouting as though the deep
ground would waken from its grim routine,

the spring soil asleep
in the bed of time, O grave and green.

This Spring

This spring I was witness once again.
I travelled by train to Des Moines
to visit my brother, but riding back
late at night I lay awake
watching the darkness when it spoke—
voices I had not heard for more than a year.

When I was a boy often I would lie
looking at the near night sky,
unaware of the arrangements of the stars
until they told me
you know who you are, you know
this is not your home. Why are you here?

The Superior Court

I wanted to study law until I listened
to the sessions of the Superior Court for Durham County
and heard the prosecuting attorney
address the jury
in the comfortable tone of a man talking
to his friends—to men
and women who might remember
days when he played baseball—
people who had seen his picture in the paper
when he was awarded his degree
upon leaving law school
and later read the report of his wedding.

The defense attorney
told the judge that he was sorry
to appear to plead for many of these people
who had promised in the past to reform
though here they stood, regardless of their word—
men sober now but still unable
to describe what drew them back
to find work at the farm
or repair the county roads under guard.
Now and then a woman taken off the street
on her fourth or fifth offense, sent away to wash
linens or learn to sew, wearing her hand-made uniform.

I wanted to practice law until I saw
how sunlight filled
the high windows of the Superior Court
every day of the spring session
while small birds made
their argument among the dogwood trees,
and the formal magnolia with large firm blossoms
trembled in the air
as a breeze brought indoors the odor
of the young grass and flowers
taking hold upon the earth so sweet and wild.

A Spring Night in Nashville

1

While we walk along the water our arms wear
the swaying air
warm as if with fever
until we turn from the Cumberland river
down a dim street and climb
to the steam of a single room.

Still the rhythm of the river
provides a pulse that throbs in the corner clubs,
in studios where the gleam of wire guitars
softens the resonance of steel

and in the evening air we feel

all songs built on the beat and tone of loneliness

but your tongue teaches music to my mouth
and our hands hear the singing of our skin.

2

A slow rain scratches the roof
when we crawl to sleep, pulling up a pale sheet.

The mind no longer lingers at the sill of the skull
but walks into the wet woods which shape one side of a
hill.

Now another leaves the body in its bed.
With such light step as not to waken man or woman
the soul too steals toward sleep beneath bleak clouds—
halts at the high window, turning to see
ourselves wrapped in one white sheet,
a cumbersome quilt across our legs
as we lie in the falling glow
of our flesh feeling surely
this is the darkness which will shelter us.
This is the night we know, in which we dream of dying,
and we die.

3
Alone the soul strolls in the night
by the full river flowing
below the cemetery of the old south,
a disparity of graves growing low in the grass
and tall tombs where the dead were sealed inside the
stones
which prolong the process of their decay.

But the ghost who goes forth from us does not regard
these silver stones in the graveyard
for more than a moment—they are not important—
does not lean long looking at the many memorial
plaques
placed in public walls, stooping to read an inscription
in the street.

Browses before the wet window
of a bookstore and sees the display of bibles;
will not buy these or other books, not maps or poems or
novels.

Perceives a patrol car cruising
the quiet neighborhood all night to note
these few men still on the street, white and black,
who walk like the soul itself without work or rest.

The warehouse guard crouches over his coffee.
His foot bounds on the bare board floor to that tune
he whistles.
One watchman on the loading dock listens
late to his radio—music floats over the freight yard.

How can the conscience of the night contain
the pain of the human heart rising in room after room?

O even in sleep our blood floods our arms;
its red rhythm stirs our skin
to open like roses, my wrist below your breast.

4
O beautiful black night when we are born
out of the distance dark and unseen
into the stillness of a city
whose streets are songs of longing
which wait for the words of our first breath.

The mind paces the porch of morning
while the spirit passes
over moist soil to its home—

The soul returns to its skin,
flowing within ourselves as the river arrives
out of the east, glowing and gliding—

O love, let us join
in the spring and be one
like the current of the Cumberland, raised by rain,
riding under the damp hills, carrying the color of the
dawn.

V

Democratic Times

The special taste which men of
democratic times entertain for
physical enjoyments. . . .

Alexis de Tocqueville,
Democracy in America

Buster Keaton
& the Cops

Stone Face is the likeness of all lovers.
Under a flower cart he keeps his seat,
hiding his hopes from the crowd
until some clown discovers
his hat in the cop-cluttered street.

The officers fall on their knees
in the flowers and find his hiding-place.
He remains undismayed.
He rubs his cuffs and dusts his collar.
The cops crawl up and greet him face to face.

He throws his roses in their eyes.
In retreat he duels for his life,
with daffodils he clouts their clubs.
He creeps from his cart and tries
to lose them in the lilies which he spills.

Then as he impeccably plucks his hat
and races through the swirling street,
his shirt-tail hangs unfurled
and waves goodbye to his heart
and goodbye to the fragrant world.

Mardi Gras

Me first
you all
the folks
tramping up
God knows
no one knows who
and our favorite dead
tramping up

everybody coming on
waving his balloon
overhead
black
orange red
anchored in his fist
floating by the least
long string

oh balls
of red white
and green blooming
up to say
it's springtime
oh say I'm
all right it's
springtime.

A Song for New Orleans

Oh the wine's fine
but listen you drink too
damn much. I drink too damn

much fine wine eating
salty fish, we have to
get out of this place

I can't whistle
you can't kiss
eating salty fish.

In the Absinthe House

Wondering how the woman in brocade can
tolerate pernod as tawny as her cheeks,
sipped over cracked ice, he turns and speaks
for her to overhear: "I should explain
that often I prefer to drink alone . . ."
She's mindful of her own designs, he suspects.
She redistributes her items and collects
her balanced buttocks on the next stool down.

"I've seen how innocence betrays a man . . ."
He hasn't enjoyed New Orleans unduly,
he tells me: "It's a damned aggravation
to arrange the afternoon so that daily
my nerves are not unstrung by the Gulf sun,
the coffee, the pernod, the shameless ladies."

On Clark Street
in Chicago

On Clark Street in Chicago
the faces that you see

are rising on the river
of immortality—

Washed by the warm water
that floods the floor of hell

they circle in the current
their voices climb and fall.

O listen when they pass us
on the sunny shore

they're calling out to Jesus
no more no more no more.

*

    Don't you ever worry
    Sugar we
    found us a place to lay—

Don't ever worry
Sugar we have
found us a place to lay—

O you give me
some sweetness, pay
you soon as I can

I'll get me my
sweetness now
here comes the honey-man.

*

On Clark Street in Chicago
your face was wet with fear

hearing the summer morning
awaking as before.

O listen to the sparrow
singing so long and clear

in the daylight slowly drying
the street outside your door—

Someone will come tomorrow
someone who wants to hear

your sweetness and your sorrow
no more no more no more.

66

November as the New Moon

November as the new moon
has begun to rise

from a field fenced only with elms
and level enough to land

in the middle of the afternoon
when a little rain rakes the brown brush
and a pack of dogs cowers on the ground,
all that barking drowned by the engine noise—

Their rumps leap up and their jaws drop
empty and
yawping below both wings.

The plane sidles down
feeling its fuselage plow
uneven into the wind, weaving to a stop.

When the rain blows off a clear freeze follows.
The moon slips out like a wedge of ice.

A dozen dogs browse by, nosing the wheels.

2

While you wait in the white grass
toward nightfall the deer
shy up the spine of the hill and veer
across a breast of the stiff meadow.

They pull the whole hill around into the trees.
When they go there's no feeling of balance,
no sense of focus once you lie down alone

like a boy basking on a raft who sees
the sky spin as he floats
around a pond.

3

The new moon
makes no motion, frozen over the silver weeds
far off, out of touch.

I can hear a small sound within a wall of trees
and the deer, undisturbed, going down in the dark
before the first snow, just beyond reach.

There's no need for a camera, flash-gun, or a good gun
still in the plane.
There's a long night
left to myself—what use to anyone?

The Hill Coast

The crew cuts in at 2:30.
By suppertime four men boost the best shark
upright, raised and roped from an iron rack
where his weight is already

a question of record. Once his body
eluded the fingering nets he bowed back
and was speared into the boat, so his trunk
was gored badly.

His trunk bagged out, water trickled out
on the boards; the boy who carved his skin
and teeth left nothing underneath the shaft

and the shore fog followed, bedding in
the blond beach and the hills and you could not
see what you saw in the water in the sun.

The Fillmore

Out to the vendor's chime
the barefoot girls
skirting the warm cement
run in dark bloom . . .
Whispering indolent
they softly bite ice cream,

legs stretched down the porchsteps
of an evening,
and see the boys approach.
But the girls tip-
toe shouting up the porch
and lick their cold sweet lips.

The Red Bluff Rodeo

They arrive
from all points in the valley—
They travel the ranch roads that connect
with paved roads feeding into the freeway
to enter town by car or truck
or on horseback,
                        all morning
the main street so full of traffic
there isn't an empty seat
in a restaurant or bar and grill
for more than a mile around the fairgrounds.

"Let me have some coffee and three eggs."
"How do you like your eggs?"
"I like 'em fine!"

*

Clowns wearing costumes
of cowboys or ranch hands
perform, falling off
the back of a plow horse
too old to mind the jeers
of spectators. One clown
climbs a cow and flings
his feet in the air,

71

slaps her rear and lifts
his eyes to the sky as though
to ask why she won't buck—
But you hear little laughter
as people slide closer
on the wooden slats,
and settle for the serious show.

*

They roar for the first rider—
What's caught the eye of the crowd
is the swift stride of his horse
and the queer stiff legs of the calf.
His lasso loops over her neck
to stop her short.
He drops beside her in the dust
and ties her legs tight with one length
of rope, and one twisted sweep of his arm.
He throws his hands in the air to show he's done,
like a man who is surrounded and forced to surrender.

Applause rattles the grandstand from its full height,
as the man and horse trot toward the gate.

The clowns come for the calf and hurry off.

Another number is announced. The chute opens. Out
flies a fresh horse, a hat, and a pair of hands
too fast for the calf
who finds herself rolling helpless
in the grip of the rope.

*

Girls squirm in the sun.
Small boys see every event
with intent eyes
until the women unwrap
sandwiches, which the children eat.
But wives who worry
whether a man will earn
as much as his entry fee
turn to each other and talk,
to ignore the noise and nervous heat.

> "Did he come home sober last night?"
> "In the dark he tripped over a chair."
> "Well what did you do?"
> "I laughed so hard I fell out of bed."

*

The last man in the saddle bronc competition
provokes a rough ride
to impress the judges.
His feet jab for flesh.

73

His spurs urge
the bronc to kick
three ways at once—

He flies from his mount
in mid-air, tossed
free. Falls
like a sack of meal in the dust.
The public disapproves and boos.
He crawls away from the hooves, on his hands and knees.

"Some sort of fun."

". . . I'm glad it's done.
All day I've been as dizzy as a squirrel."

The crowd staggers out of the stands,
pressing into the parking lot.

Evening dresses the country in cool stars.

Far in the night a fitful line of light
searches the length of the valley,
where families follow one another home
beyond the lost barns and deserted fields.

Charlie Chaplin Has the Last Laugh

The scene suggests a city full of schemes.
The Tramp taps his cane tip-pat tip-pat
and lolls by a lamppost looking at his shoes.
His pants are a bag of dreams.

His landlord flaps his fat chins on his collar,
strutting down the street like a side of beef.
He wears a bulge of banknotes in his hips
and a smile like the crease in a fresh dollar.

A smile that drips with malice when he trips over
someone's cane
and gathers himself in a gutter
where the rainwater runs in a river

and the Tramp stares at his feet feeling shy
at such success.
Left with his thumbing luck
he buttons his ravelled vest to his fly.

He limps by like a man bent with bundles.
His black breast curves like a crow's,
but his wax white eyes
flicker flicker as innocent as candles.

VI

What Is the Wild Love that Leads Us?

If we could first know *where* we are, and *wither* we are tending, we could then better judge *what* to do, and *how* to do it.

Abraham Lincoln

After His Assassination a Place of Peace

After his assassination a place of peace,
a church
impatient with piety,
pleas for Kennedy—
"Receive, receive, your servant Jack."
Long lines of mourners murmur and turn back.
St. John's belfry wheel winds, and unreels its chimes.

The amber lamps upon the roof
of the radio tower pulse on and off.
Throughout the hour
wire reports grow like fine steel vines.

Thru this electric speech a siren climbs
above the trees and screams
for the body borne away,
given to the grass.

Poor death, beggaring death
seeking a gift of us
that has our breath.

In our restless peace
what can my hand touch
that will bloom? Or our arms reach
that will bear?

2

Wind warps the shingled roofs slanting by the green
City Plaza where boughs storm;
winter oranges blaze like Christmas balls.

The green sign
of Christ will twine,
Love's wreath
cut from the tree of our wrath.

Everywhere we watch for this certainty.

The rain wells in the crotch
of a walnut tree.

3

Water slides off a purple rib of the foothills,
lifting silt;
washes west on the slow brush floor
and into the milling Sacramento
quietly spills.

4

Grief goes open in the street . . .
If we kill,
Sweet Christ,
who are free,
then where is our peace?

What burns my blood away
in my own flesh?

          Doves cower asleep
          dry in the crowns
          of green palms.

On the black airfield a radar cup waits.
Lights wink with power, clicking rise
along a low cloudbank, begin
their sweeping spin,
and death's found
day and night in each town;
O come under the drifting skies . . .

The valley rain chills your skin
and distracts and turns your dead
legs, and your spirit dead, growing into the winter of
    the war.

November carries cold across the land
an inconstant sun . . . the sand coasts gripped in ice.

5

Night nods beside the road but will not sleep.
A time to map the madness that destroys a man.

On the carved wall, car lights search the canyon fog
and find the blind bend, and begin dimming down,
floating up the road toward town.

6

Dawn rises in the streets of our unrest.

Notes drop from the apartment of a pianist.
People in the plaza stop to listen,
caught by the cold strain
of music this morning,
as though memory might admire a deliberate refrain.

7

A raw rain pours and stains
the skinned sycamores.

The rain crawls in the street, it looks insane,
it sits there, at noon, unclean
licked by dogs.

South in the valley a late yield
is marginal. Water grass
eats the profits out of the rice field.

All of these things are so, this is the way
they are seen.

But there is a deep disorder now
between the eye and brain.

There is a deep disorder, a ditch between
what you can see
and what you can reach, and touch:

the ordinary darkness
of human figures of men or women,
the company of others coming out on the river ground,

walking on a drying slope, overlooking the high water,
blades of wood awash in the mud-silt seeping
under a boat landing, and swelling down into the delta.

8

The wet air gleams. After the rain

the sunlight is planked by a blue shade
that moves. A human
figure, man or woman,
a shadow-shape the sun casts in the grass.

So my spirit's sorrow
returns to town, unable
to follow its friend further, as the shadow
of my flesh falls before me.

9

Jets cross the missle silos, and a bluff low
on the unchanneled salmon water,
and ride tandem, then divide

while the wind booming the boughs
buries its breath in a pool.
After the rain all of these things are so—
on the road leaves spawn and litter and stream

in a flash chill like the first
frost on a ranch banked in blossoms;
late warnings are broadcast, the alert lamps smoke in
    the orchards.

Though disaster and death drive us out
of the solitary city
or town or prairie
we bring in our blood
all the joy and anguish which we see.

Our blest blood gains from the spirit the speed
of a child,
                grace in the veins,
the birds' timing—

A schoolboy fields a punt,
slips a tackler,
and he's free.

In the ranch air
and the deep farmland
the doves complain and hunt.

Small Moon on the Shoulder of New York

Small moon on the shoulder of New York.
In an alley children swim
against the dark. Some drift home.

Others remain among the stairs
and green garage doors,

not one window lighted by a bulb
while they prolong their game,
choosing to search or sit hidden

in the narrow night. An hour later
the full moon on the rise

will find them here, with its white eyes.
It finds my hands! My hair!
Hangs in my heart like a large lamp,

leaving no shadow to hide your eyes
or the orb of each breast—

You occupy my mind like the moon!
The same light lands everywhere
outside the alley. The street corner

where a couple kiss before they cross
to the park. Pale moon light

on the trees like water turns the leaves
to snow. This glow chills
my skin when I lie down alone—

The grass! The grass! Why is it so cold?
The long white grass of the moon—

Lines on Eliot's Death

Always by water, by a rock-burst high and wet
he came to value
the earth's weather. Always by water

surf blowing near Cape Ann
or the ocean boiling,
scrubbing at Europe's paralytic body

at the starved figures of men waiting
for the love of a god in a woman
or upon a man's mind—

the long waves flooding, washing men who wait
for the power on the tide that will move
and will come to drown the man who stands too late—

He walked there, watched there, wrote home
of the green tide, flaking sea-foam
as raw as a prairie snow. But turning home

along the baking street you are
aware of men's speech, of a cathedral air
in the heart, and the rational blasphemies.

> Christ speaks as a man
> God made, and cries down dying,
> lifted down before nightfall.

Mind and body rage against their age
and remain obedient to the laws
inscribed in our blood.

Once only is the fall
sun in fever with memory
of the surf blowing in, to Cape Ann

        when a tall girl
        unfolds a basket
        on the sloping shade,

        in the compacted day
        white roots, blades
        and branches halt.

The rivers freeze with rot
frozen in them, the waterways brown and hard
like summer roads.

        The sand light is clear,
sunlight brinks the regretful waterways,
then evening chills the beach air

and the turning of a cold year
lulls and waits now
lost London inters him in her winter spirit.

The Statute of Limitations

The first snow of October slows travel
on the road to Terezin. Guards
by the gate build a fire,
waiting for the trucks
heavy with children coming into camp.

Sparks of snow burn on the cement ramp.
The children delivered
from the trucks flock
down the cold platform,
crowding together at the gate.

In one snowbound field a fence bends
on the border of the pine fertile night.
From the federal forest a flat light crawls
on the ground where the moon
has found a way to enter through the trees.

Wires and slats sink from sight,
boundaries buried under the weight of winter.
Nothing is seen of the perimeter of Dachau
before a liberating thaw
in April raises the rivers loud and green.

All the radios are humming like boxes of bees.
A beacon probes the fish-like blue
and white bellies of the strike planes.
A major anti-morale mission.
Smoke obscures the sky from any vision.

2

Our peace is political.
After a complete generation
like a chilled organism the heart
contracts.
The drawing-room is the tomb of the lyric.

This placid cold
surface seals the soul
like a lake locked in ice.
Abstract politics control
the exuberance of art—

Luckless in love on Christmas eve
Mozart fled to the banquet hall
to embrace a new romance,
casting off his claret coat
to join the girls and drink and dance!

3

Politic nations know
a compliant man
by the relaxed grasp
of his hand. All
its fingers folding like a shell.

A man who has developed
a taste for death.
Old mouth with no teeth.
Voice saying someone will
understand, will understand.

4

In Bonn a man
whose crime justifies
his silence in the hushed salon—
a man the age of our fathers
outlives many shadows

buried in the yellow meadow
where good friends gather close at hand.
Now in his mature days the sun's rays glare
along the red street. He retreats
from his name as sunlight gleams

over steel rails. In the rocking
room he reads briefly. Sleeps and dreams
of a woman. Awakens with a lurch.
Leaving the steam-warm compartment of his coach,
he grips his gear and departs, stepping

from the train to voices drifting
down the white slopes prepared
for the last week of winter sport,
strolling among young couples
at a Bavarian resort.

As dusk approaches, chilling, blue,
the ski jumpers poise
and swoop,
the last one to lift off
leaning below a few ashen clouds . . .

> He is free to fly!
> He is free!
> His soul leaps and soars
> into the long evening sky,
> pursued by the flaming stars.

The Wind

When the wind cries winter we stop and listen
    to that tone of voice as stiff as ice.
Snow has left the city its own color,
    while a cold silence closes every ear.

When the wind calls spring we walk the street
    beside the black Chicago river,
where flags on a few boats blossom in the air.
    It promises robins and we believe what we hear.

A Song for Salt Lake

When we left the city behind
we could find no trace
of a breeze— It had gone
across the water only
a breath on the unbroken shine
of a summer night—
                          Alone
on the white shore we saw
the naked mountains shiver
while the dry heat of day
withdrew in the dark.

The tide turned out
which made the shore appear
to feel the planet's pull.
Water flowed
toward a far light
like the surface of a mirror.

How near you were, how still
we lay while we
looked out on this lake
where we saw the scars
that mark the mild face
of our neighbor moon,
who moves us more
than all the scattered stars.

The Big
Rock Candy Mountain

I

The swift breeze baffles
the bees.
Drunk in the nectar breeze
bees pester the evergreens.
Honey hangs in the limbs.

Axes ring
and falling in the sweet green air
the pines explode on the mountain slope.
The saws bite and slice the singing air.

And the beef and black beer forever at dusk
and the camp wives waiting in the ice clear night.

2

Down U.S. 80, jeeps
trail the munitions trucks to the coast.
The slow brown trucks burn west
like a fire lane scorched on the prairie.
On the Pacific rails flat-cars carry
cannon and rocketry to the cargo ships.
A good sleep, cold, fast as the stream
running on the rock-bed.

3

Morning, and now the circle saw rips, and now
the breeze swarms the limbs,
bees swim in the humming dust
of dreams.

> In the full sun we grope
> hand to hand, waking, on the cool west shelf.
> High in the cutting slope
> the bees hum in the sweet dust.
> We dream, we dream.

Speech of the
Dead Pilot's Spirit

Let my mother lead the line
where the box borne from the belly of the plane
is hauled on a handtruck to its rest.
My father might unfold the red and white
stripes of the flag which shine
with history, while harsh sunlight
strikes the strip. A few friends remain
alert in that heat to hear the last
argument uttered by an anxious ghost.

No one will die
to deserve your grief.
When the girl I loved left school
with me one morning, we cruised up and down
the coast in my car. Evening saw us lie
on a small bend of beach below town.
Twilight lasted long but the nights were brief—
at dawn the sheep on one high hill
behind our backs would wake us with their call.

My mind kept to that cove where we slept.
I was so naive I never feared
the future. Only a week later

she met a young man in Monterey,
and they were married. We ought to accept
what we're worth. When she left me that day
my life was over, and I volunteered.
Earth is as empty as the sky—without her
would I be happy? Then what does it matter?

The Sheep

On a green morning in spring we step out
a few feet at a time, stooping to eat
the top of the growing hill.
Beyond the end of each town
like the poor we are here at the edge
of everyone's sight, where we bow our heads
to the ground, going on with our meal.

2

We stand in the sun and eat thru the summer.
Our coats are the color of untreated clay.
We are the sheep the children see night and day.
They want to feel our fleece,
they want to hear what happens to all our wool.
Does it hurt to clip it? How fast will it grow? How
   does it smell?

3

Each morning in fall we eat the cool hill
before the highway traffic appears.
Pairs of headlights reach into the rain
while tall trucks follow the cars which whine
past the posted signs—
                    For years

the land has been up for sale,
but no buyers. The soil
too dry in summer
and wet all winter.

4

Let winter arrive we are ready
to outwait every trouble man knows—
snow in the foothills, a flood in the valley,
or the freezing spell that turns his wells to ice—
with no thought for his grief, happy in this life,
alone with our own hunger and as lasting as the grass.

The Land of the Dead

A shimmer of summer
heat haunts the county road before dark.
The cars rattle flat out, level with the red land,
and skid down the dusty grade
to stop by the pines;
the doors clap open
and the men climb out,
slipping away from the warm fear of America.

The scrub pine
fills a forest as green as rain;
on the riverbed
of red clay, the grass has gone to seed.

From here men have escaped
to the other world,
the land of the dead.
Their bodies disappear
down a grassy rise,
the eyes of their souls
look back and see the moon
like a barge, built with bones, floating on the field.

And more black men sit whispering
on the fishing pier

with their lines strung in the river,
boat and oars
half hid downshore
and the moon rowing over the grass forever.

With King in Memphis

With King in Memphis marching
behind the wide line
of black dignitaries
a wave of white students
overtakes a few dozen
striking black men
while the new nuns come
unconfined by their habits,
no white wimples hiding
their temples, like old world
war one pilots striding
among a pack of priests.
Herding them into rows,
the parade marshals hurry
past the police and carry
their portable radios
proudly like pieces of cake.
But welfare workers join
with journalists and jostle
the crowd of jobless colored
people and the slow passing
pensioners. In the wake
of the throng walks a chain
of girls who were let out
of a local convent school

to entertain the others
with a song. Each one wears
her blue blouse and subdued skirt
of blue and grey squares,
and once the long sea
of people pauses fitfully
they hold hands and sing:

"Friends of our Lord
we come your way
thru the weary world
that grows so dim,
that we may pray
for you, and you,
to bring a prayer
to pawn for Him
and sing with us
this song today
so God will bless
all in distress.

Our Lord will raise
the widow's eyes
from the quiet floor
and will make gay
the orphan's voice
at play once more;
He hears your cry
and will most heed
with His rich love

the hunger of
the poor, the poor
now, in their need."

Alone on the top step
of the public library
looking deserted and sleepy
a black activist in
a jet black bike jacket
wags his sign: *Whitey
Deserves to Die!* Curled
beneath his feet a girl
watches the men marching by,
rocks her chin on her knees,
locks her fingers around
her brown ankles, but nothing
she sees stirs her until
there's no hope of escape.
She flies up the stairs
by the boy at the door
as the police pour across
the curb, into the crowd,
and a young squad races up
the street, chasing the women
in retreat, wheeling them on
their heels, hearing them scream
before a dreamlike fear
of drowning leaves them calling
out and floods their faces,
and still they cannot stop

the beating of their blood
that makes the young men leap
like drunken dancers falling,
like dead men going down
again and again in the warm
waves of their dark voices.

You Are Never Happy

America, you are never happy, and slowly
the season freezes like a lake in heaven.
Leaves unfold flying in a blizzard blowing
wings of yellow wax to garment the grass.

There are shapeless weights in the weather all winter.
You are never happy, yesterday you thought
about the thickness of things that have no bark
or handles no you are never happy.

You are worried when the sunlight leans uneasy
and understanding the State Department
is like moving mattresses, you are never happy,
there are shapeless weights in the weather all winter.

The cherry trees refuse to freeze at the close
of Congress, they remember Lincoln angry
at last, lunging at Seward and saying,
"Any man over forty is responsible for his face!"

Slowly the time forms like ice in heaven
where saints skate shaving off the domes of the clouds,
sending us snow spraying down all day
on white wings of wax though you are never happy.

Look You're Laughing

Look you're laughing when we point out the prints
the cougar made, the mark of each paw
preserved in fresh snow . . . The four firm
toes are spread no wider than my palm.
Yet you can almost feel the force
of her high flanks and chest that pressed them so.

Desperate in winter, driven by hunger, the female
snuck into camp at dusk, sniffing the smoke,
pretending to be about other business
as she took a bedroll by one stray corner
between her teeth, shook it, let it go
and leaped away on the long white slope,

the blur of her brown and rust colored coat in the mind
of everyone talking at once, telling what you missed.
Look you're laughing but if you saw the cat
creeping over to pull at your pillow,
then we could show other people the shallow tracks
you left behind, your feet hardly even touching the
    snow.

'Time Accomplishes
for the Poor What Money
Does for the Rich'

—CESAR CHAVEZ

They sit on the windy sidewalk waiting
to enjoy a joke. No matter how many times
they have seen this they never grow
tired of watching the ritual
which is performed every morning.

Twin limousines glide together and stop
traffic momentarily in the middle of both lanes.
The governor looks grim as he leans
from the rear door of one and climbs
into the other, changing cars ...

Partly superstition, partly precaution.
From the front seat his guard
observes the Mexicans who sit
on the walk outside the bars
and furniture stores on Folsom Boulevard.

Under swollen sycamores and tall palm trees
both vehicles continue toward the capitol,
pursuing one another thru the traffic.
Since they are identical it is impossible
to say in which one he will arrive today,

until he emerges and his fine hair is blown
in the wind, the wind that blows tomorrow
and the next night and
the next day when we will all eat
the bread in our hands and we will all drink wine.

Geese Going North

They fight to be free of our earth,
legs dangling, drawn up in the driving air,
wings stroking the wind, beating its current beneath the
    keel
of the breastbone as they're borne
toward that loud height
where we find them this morning in full flight.

On an April morning they ride
our warm wind from the south,
so many that all I can hear is their cry—
Canada Geese and Blues and Snows,
thousands squawking in the sky
while they flash over fields that weathered the winter.

On into noon they pass
in formation along the flyway
before they flock down to feed,
attracted by acres of corn or barley
and eager to graze on fresh grain or grass.
Once more they climb on the wind

and soar like a man who has flown
free of his thought,
happy to shed his shadow,

his dark image drifting alone
on swift wings over the earth. Wings which carry
the clamorous speed of the birds

farther than eyes can listen
for their long calls flying
out of the day and the fecund land
where our flesh follows.
As though to enclose the cool lake lying
below their voices

a pine forest grows
more green and remote when it rises.
Geese glide thru these trees to reach the shore.
At rest on the water, wide wings withdrawn,
they float over the lake in its last light,
blue pool of the soul that deepens with the night.

What Is the Wild Love that Leads Us?

What is the wild love that leads us down
to the end of the flat canyon floor,
cluttered with leaves and branches blown
to earth and rotting in the rain,

and urges us onto this trail,
tracking for mile after mile?
The rain holds behind us until
we stumble to find our footing where

we've waded into the iron cold snow
that all but covers a mountain meadow.
What is the wild love that leads us far
away from the long land below,

the hunt forgotten in the autumn air
full of flakes? By dark the storm
has died down and we see moonlight bloom
across the ridge. But when we climb

beyond the prints of the small brown bear
and the last clean tracks of the deer
and fall into a circle by the fire,
what is the wild love that leads us here?